Prince William

ABDO
Publishing Company

by **Sarah Tieck**

Published by ABDO Publishing Company, 8000 West 78th Street, Edina, Minnesota 55439.

Printed in the United States of America, North Mankato, Minnesota.
062011
112011

 PRINTED ON RECYCLED PAPER

Coordinating Series Editor: Rochelle Baltzer
Contributing Editors: Megan M. Gunderson, BreAnn Rumsch, Marcia Zappa
Graphic Design: Maria Hosley
Cover Photograph: *AP Photo*: John Stillwell/PA Wire URN:9893578 (Press Association via AP Images).
Interior Photographs/Illustrations: *AP Photo*: AP Photo (p. 9), British Library/PA Wire URN:6954476 (Press Association via AP Images) (p. 9), Hugo Burnand (p. 23), David Caulkin (p. 7), David Cheskin, Pool (p. 17), John Gaps III, file (p. 14), Alastair Grant, Pool (p. 17), PA (p. 13), Lefteris Pitarakis (p. 22), Press Association via AP Images (p. 21), John Stillwell, Pool (p. 25), Kirsty Wigglesworth (p. 21), Kirsty Wigglesworth/PA Wire URN:10622703 (Press Association via AP Images) (p. 29); *Getty Images*: Jayne Fincher (p. 11), Tim Graham (p. 13), Indigo (p. 27), Chris Jackson (p. 4), ROTA (p. 19); *Glow Images*: Antique Research Centre (p. 9).

Library of Congress Cataloging-in-Publication Data

Tieck, Sarah, 1976-
  Prince William : real-life prince / Sarah Tieck.
    p. cm. -- (Big buddy biographies)
  ISBN 978-1-61783-022-8
  1. William, Prince, grandson of Elizabeth II, Queen of Great Britain, 1982---Juvenile literature. 2. Princes--Great Britain--Biography--Juvenile literature. I. Title.
  DA591.A45W55844 2011
  941.086092--dc22
  [B]
                          2011017209

Prince
William

Contents

Prince William got the title of Duke of Cambridge on his wedding day. It was a gift from his grandmother, Queen Elizabeth II.

Future King

Prince William, Duke of Cambridge, is a real-life prince. He is the oldest son of Charles, Prince of Wales. This makes him second in line to be king of England.

Scotland

NORTH SEA

Northern Ireland

UNITED KINGDOM

ATLANTIC OCEAN

IRELAND

Wales

England
London

Family Ties

Prince William was born in London, England, on June 21, 1982. His full name is William Arthur Philip Louis Windsor.

William grew up in London as part of England's royal family. His parents are Charles and Diana, Prince and Princess of Wales. His younger brother is Prince Harry.

Prince Charles married Lady
Diana Spencer on July 29, 1981.
More than 750 million people
watched the event on television.

William was very close to his mother.
Diana was well liked by the public.

Royal Roots

England has almost always had a king or queen. This position passes from parents to children. Some queens or kings have no children. Then, another family member is chosen.

Over the years, different families have ruled England. Some of the kings and queens are still very famous! As king someday, William will be part of royal history.

Queen Elizabeth II is William's grandmother. She became queen of England in 1952.

Henry VIII was a famous king of England in the early 1500s. He started the Church of England.

Queen Victoria ruled England from 1837 to 1901. During this time, there was much growth in science and books.

Growing Up

As England's **future** king, William needed a good education. So, he attended schools for talented students. He studied at Wetherby School in London. Next, he went to Ludgrove School.

William liked school and earned good grades. He also enjoyed sports such as **polo** and swimming.

In 1995, William began attending Eton College. It is a school for boys ages 13 to 18.

In 1992, William's parents separated. William and Harry spent time with each of their parents. They visited the countryside with their father. Together, they practiced shooting, fishing, and riding horses.

William's mother took them with her to homeless shelters and hospitals. She also let them do things like ordinary kids. Together, they visited Walt Disney World and ate at McDonald's.

William and Harry hiked in the countryside with their father.

William and Harry enjoyed spending time with their mother.

13

> William walked behind his mother's coffin. His brother, father, uncle, and grandfather stood beside him.

Did you know...

People said William was very brave and strong during his mother's funeral.

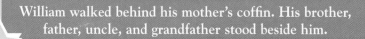

Saying Good-bye

In 1996, William's parents divorced. Then in 1997, William's life changed when his mother died in a car crash. William and Harry were very sad to lose her.

Princess Diana was no longer officially part of the royal family. But, she was honored with a royal funeral.

Military Man

In 2001, William began attending the University of Saint Andrews in Scotland. There he studied art history and **geography**. He **graduated** in 2005.

Next, William studied at the Royal Military Academy Sandhurst. He finished in 2006. Later, he joined the Royal Air Force and the Royal Navy. Someday when he is king, he will be the head of England's military.

In 2008, William became a knight in the Most Noble Order of the Garter. This is a special honor in England.

Working Together

During her life, Princess Diana spent time helping others. She taught William and Harry to do this, too. After her death, they continued much of her work. Both William and Harry help people and **charities**.

William and Kate dated for many years before getting married.

A Royal Wedding

In 2010, William asked his girlfriend, Kate Middleton, to marry him. People around the world were excited about the couple's engagement.

Like William, Kate graduated from the University of Saint Andrews. Then, she worked as a fashion buyer. She also helped with her family's business.

William gave Kate his mother's engagement ring. It has diamonds around a large blue gem.

After the wedding, William and Kate kissed on the balcony of Buckingham Palace. William's parents had done the same on their wedding day!

William and Kate's wedding took place in London on April 29, 2011. They were married at Westminster Abbey.

The event drew much attention. About 1 million people lined the streets of London to watch. Millions more watched the event on television and the Internet.

William and Kate's families
came together for the wedding.

23

A Prince's Life

As a **future** king, Prince William has a different life from most people. He and Kate attend many events as part of the royal family. They have guards to keep them safe.

William and Kate have a house in the countryside in Wales. William is serving there as part of the Royal Air Force until 2013. He and Kate want a normal life. So William drives himself to work, and they cook their own meals.

After their wedding, William and Kate were called the Duke and Duchess of Cambridge.

Travel is also a part of William's busy life.
He and Kate go to London for events. And,
they visit Africa and the Caribbean
for fun.

The couple also visits the royal family's
homes, such as Windsor Castle. And,
William enjoys spending time at his father's
farm. There, he works with sheep and pigs.

Since William married Kate, people are even more interested in their lives.

Buzz

Prince William is learning to do the work of a king. He attends events, travels the world, and does military work.

People are excited to see what's next for Prince William. Many believe he has a bright **future** as the king of England.

Snapshot

★ **Name**: Prince William Arthur Philip Louis Windsor

★ **Birthday**: June 21, 1982

★ **Birthplace**: London, England

★ **Schools**: Wetherby School, Ludgrove School, Eton College, University of Saint Andrews, Royal Military Academy Sandhurst

★ **Official Titles**: Duke of Cambridge, Earl of Strathearn, Baron Carrickfergus

Important Words

charity a group or a fund that helps people in need.

engagement (ihn-GAYJ-muhnt) an agreement to someday get married.

future (FYOO-chuhr) a time that has not yet occurred.

geography (jee-AH-gruh-fee) the study of places, cultures, and living things on Earth and how they are related to each other.

graduate (GRA-juh-wayt) to complete a level of schooling.

polo a team sport played on horseback.

Web Sites

To learn more about Prince William, visit ABDO Publishing Company online. Web sites about Prince William are featured on our Book Links page. These links are routinely monitored and updated to provide the most current information available.

www.abdopublishing.com

Index

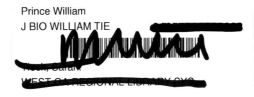